THE CHICAGO INFERNO

THE CHICAGO INFERNO

Charles R. Boning

Illustrated by

Joseph Forte

The Incredible Series

Barnell Loft, Ltd., Baldwin, New York

To

the public and private schools

of the city of Chicago

It was a warm, breezy night in the bustling city of Chicago. A lecturer, Francis Train, was speaking in Farwell Hall, an auditorium near the center of the city. The talk wasn't going well. Train knew he needed to say something dramatic to attract the fading attention of the restless audience. Suddenly an idea came to him. He raised his voice and predicted: "This is the last public address that will be delivered within these walls. A terrible calamity is impending over the city of Chicago! More I cannot say; more I dare not utter!" The listeners were now wide awake. A few shifted nervously in their chairs. Most snickered and coughed in disbelief.

A hot, dry summer had parched Chicago during that year of 1871. Trees had withered under the endless glare of the sun. For three weeks now, there hadn't been a sprinkle of rain. Even for several months before, there had been just a few drops. Now a thin layer of choking dust was settling over the entire city.

Numerous fires had begun to erupt throughout Chicago because of the drought. The fire department had been working long hours to contain and conquer these blazes. By now firefighters were beginning to tire under the tremendous strain.

Shortly after Train's startling forecast, strangely
enough, a major fire broke out on the West Side of town.
Thousands of excited onlookers gazed at the blaze from
street level. Others, who wanted more spectacular views,
climbed into the branches of trees or gathered on nearby
roofs. Even though nearly every piece of fire equipment
in the city was summoned to help put out the fire, it
continued to spread. Several blocks of houses and
factories were gutted before the south branch of the
Chicago River finally blocked the fire's rampage.

Front-page headlines spread word of the costly blaze. The *Chicago Tribune,* a popular newspaper, warned, "The absence of rain for three weeks has left everything in so dry and inflammable a condition that a spark might start a fire which would sweep from end to end of the city." Chicago's one-third of a million citizens were not overly concerned. In spite of the grim warning, they felt secure in the knowledge that the two rivers which divided the city into three sections formed natural barriers. Besides, on the South Side, many of the buildings were massive stone structures. Surely they could resist any fire.

Who of sound mind would ever believe that the unlikely prediction of Francis Train and the warning in the *Chicago Tribune* would soon come true? Who would possibly dream that the very next night, Sunday, October 8, 1871, was to become the most memorable date in the history of Chicago?

Irene Schmidt, who worked in Field and Leiter's Department Store, had an out-of-town visitor, Kate Herbst, staying at her home. Irene was eager to impress her guest with the city's many exciting sights, such as the Chamber of Commerce and Crosby's Opera House. Beaming with pride, Irene spent Sunday showing Kate the fancy marble courthouse, the many stately hotels, imposing banks, and magnificent stores. Soon it was twilight. The two young women were ready for a warm supper and some much-needed sleep. Monday would arrive all too soon, and once again Irene would be on her way to her job at the department store.

In the crowded slums on the West Side of Chicago lived an Irish-American family named O'Leary. Behind the O'Learys' wooden shanty was their barn, which housed several cows and other animals. It was shortly after 8:30 on this tinder-dry evening that a neighbor, Daniel Sullivan, spied flames flickering from the side of the barn. As fast as he could with his one good leg, Daniel hobbled toward the burning building shouting, "Fire! Fire!"

Legend says that one of the O'Leary cows kicked over a lantern. Actually neither Daniel Sullivan nor anyone else ever knew how the fire started. But within minutes the barn was a roaring pillar of flame. From that moment, the name O'Leary was forever linked to the disastrous Chicago Fire—the one blaze against which all future fires would be measured.

Near the center of Chicago stood the courthouse. From its dome one could look down upon nearly the entire city. From this lofty perch, the firewatcher, Mathias Schafer, could spot even a small and distant fire. Mathias was chatting with some friends, when one of them pointed to a small glow in the west. At first Mathias dismissed the glow. "Nothing out of the ordinary," he muttered. "Probably just the usual light from the gasworks." But soon his mistake became apparent. Leaping flames began to silhouette the roofs of buildings near the fire. Now alarmed, he told the dispatcher downstairs the location of the blaze. Immediately, the dispatcher notified the fire department. Then it dawned on Mathias. He had given the wrong location! The fire wasn't even close to where he had said it was! Now panicking, he ran downstairs to persuade the dispatcher to send the fire department to the new location—the correct one. The dispatcher stubbornly refused.

"That would only cause more confusion," the dispatcher maintained. Mathias pleaded. But as the two men argued, the fire spread.

The dull ringing of the courthouse bell had alerted the city that yet another fire had broken out. The city's fire marshal, Robert Williams, was sound asleep, still exhausted from fighting the previous evening's fire. Awakened by his wife, he jumped into his uniform. Within minutes, his private coach rolled up. He and his driver raced through the streets toward the glow that was lighting the sky. By the time Robert Williams reached the scene, almost a full block was engulfed. The few fire companies already there were waging a losing battle against the crackling flames. Only those crews who had actually seen the blaze were on hand! The fire marshal kept asking himself, "Where are the other crews? What could've happened to them?" He had no way of knowing about the firewatcher's and dispatcher's errors.

Despite the ever-advancing flames, the firefighters were encouraged by Fire Marshal Williams' arrival. He was well-liked and known for his skill in directing his forces. His black beard, youthful face, and broad shoulders were familiar to every one of the city's 190 firefighters.

Finally more fire companies began to pull up. Williams barked orders through his brass speaking trumpet. The crews quickly followed directions. It was beginning to look as if the fire might be halted after all.

But then Fire Marshal Williams' heart sank. He saw that the water pressure was failing. Worse still, the wind was beginning to pick up. A bad sign—a very bad sign! Glancing overhead, Marshal Williams shuddered. Flaming shingles and embers, carried by the wind, were landing on roofs all over the neighborhood.

Frightened citizens quickly grabbed a few prized possessions and ran in terror from their homes. More and more desperate people poured into the streets in wild flight from the burning section of the city.

Time after time, the firefighters were forced to retreat. At every turn they battled to stem the hungry flames. They prayed that they would be able to stop the destruction of a large portion of the West Side. Just then a messenger ran up to Fire Marshal Williams shouting, "The flaming embers are jumping the river! Now the South Side's on fire!"

The whole Chicago skyline took on an orange glow. The city was bathed in an eerie light, nearly as brilliant as the noonday sun. The flames, driven by the wind, leaped higher and higher. Even the largest and sturdiest structures proved to be no match for the onrushing fire. The "fireproof" courthouse and the sparkling new Grand Pacific Hotel were swallowed by flames. Employees of the *Chicago Tribune* fought to keep their building from falling victim to the raging blaze. They scurried about on the roof, frantically trying to put out small fires the moment they started. Soon, though, the situation grew dangerous. Windowpanes cracked from the intense heat. Even the finish on furniture near the windows began to blister and smoke. "Abandon the building!" the defenders of the *Tribune* were told. "There's little time left!"

In the post office, Alanzo Mannis, a clerk, worked rapidly to save the mail. Every few moments he peered nervously out the windows behind him at the flames drawing nearer and nearer. Just before the building burned, he ran from it carrying one last sack of mail. Alanzo's chest heaved as he struggled to drag the heavy bundle to a place of safety.

Could Alanzo trust anyone to look after the sack until he returned with a wagon? He spied a woman sitting next to a pile of possessions she had saved. Alanzo asked her if she would guard the sack. Sitting upon it, the woman bravely declared, "If anyone attempts to take the mail, I will shoot him on the spot."

By now the streets were choked with terrified Chicagoans. Crazed horses ran blindly, knocking down everyone in their paths. Scurrying rats, driven from their holes and nests, were trampled under the feet of the surging crowds. Drunks staggered in circles, not knowing that their time on earth was fast running out. Some, before they knew enough to flee, were encircled by the searing heat. One by one they surrendered to the flames with pitiful screams.

People trapped in upper stories of burning buildings faced a cruel choice: jump to their deaths or perish in the flames. High above the milling crowd, a man appeared in a window. As the onlookers gaped upwards, he quietly prepared to leap. Some turned away to avoid seeing his fatal plunge. Then a roar arose from those still watching. Incredibly, the man had caught hold of the ledge below. A wave of hope ran through the crowd. Again he dropped, and again he grabbed the next ledge. The crowd cheered wildly. In just a few moments the daring man would be safe.

Once more he repeated his amazing stunt. This time his bleeding fingers lost their desperate grip. Down, down he plummeted, arms clutching frantically at the air. A hero an instant ago, the man now lay limp and broken in the dirt—like a doll that some angry child might have thrown to the ground.

Building after building was enveloped in sheets of flame. Whirlwinds of fire swept across the city. The heat of the inferno caused stone to chip and explode. Even steel beams and girders melted. Some of the largest and most majestic buildings disappeared in minutes.

Fire Marshal Williams was told that help was on its way. Fire equipment was being rushed by train to Chicago from nearby cities. It seemed too good to be true. But then Williams suddenly realized that it would all be too late—much too late. His beloved Chicago would be in ashes long before the equipment could be put to use.

On the North Side, most people still felt confident that they were not in danger. Neighbors noticed with curiosity that Richard Bellinger, a police officer, was clearing away anything that could burn from around his new home. "What a waste of time," one woman chuckled. "The fire will never reach this section of the city!" Just the same, Richard would take no chances. He and his brother-in-law were worried by the brightness of the distant flames and the direction of the wind. Richard had just had the house constructed for his wife. Now, he and his brother-in-law were ready to defend it at all costs.

Elsewhere in Chicago, city leaders, near despair, grasped at one last plan to halt the fire. James Hildreth, a retired politician, urged the mayor, Roswell Mason, to allow him to blow up rows of buildings before the flames could reach them. With no buildings in its path, the fire would have little to feed on. Mayor Mason agreed that it would be worth a try.

The boom of the explosions and the thunder of collapsing buildings echoed above the howling wind and roaring fire. Hundreds of people turned to watch as the flames approached the wrecked buildings. Would the fire stop there? In a short time the question would be answered. At first the flames seemed just to nibble on the partially demolished buildings. But in minutes the fire picked up speed and reached the other side of the ruins. The plan had failed.

By now everyone—from city leaders to ordinary citizens—realized that the flames could not be stopped. Only one question remained. Could anything at all be saved from the seething ocean of fire?

Just as Richard Bellinger feared, the fire reached the North Side. As the flames approached his home, Richard and his brother-in-law covered the roof with water-drenched rugs.

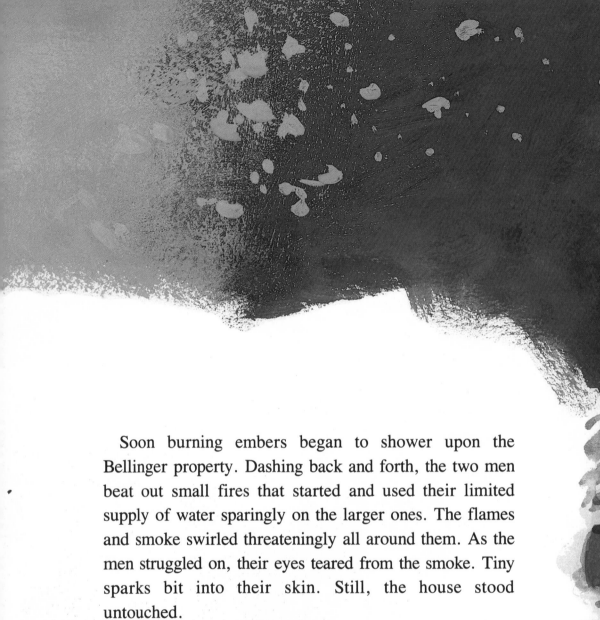

Soon burning embers began to shower upon the Bellinger property. Dashing back and forth, the two men beat out small fires that started and used their limited supply of water sparingly on the larger ones. The flames and smoke swirled threateningly all around them. As the men struggled on, their eyes teared from the smoke. Tiny sparks bit into their skin. Still, the house stood untouched.

Then Richard realized that his water supply was almost gone. His mind searched furiously for a solution. There just had to be a way to save his beautiful little home. Then he remembered. In his cellar was a keg of apple cider. Using the cider for water, the men were able to fend off the flames. The Bellinger house would stand for many years as a tribute to their courageous efforts.

It was Monday morning, October 9. Irene Schmidt, the young employee of Field & Leiter's Department Store, was hurrying to work from her home in the distant suburbs of the West Side. She couldn't afford to be late.

Irene had slept peacefully, completely unaware of the tragedy that was occurring. Despite her rush, she noticed something strange: droves of tattered-looking people were sitting about on heaps of personal belongings. As she walked through areas untouched by the fire, she became aware of a smoky haze drifting through the streets. What could possibly have happened?

Rounding a corner near the Lake Street Bridge, Irene froze in horror. Her city was gone! Chicago—only yesterday the fourth largest city in the nation—was no longer there. The wide, tree-lined streets—the tall, proud buildings—all were gone.

Here and there a shattered wall jutted above the smoking rubble. In the distance great columns of fire still shot into the sky. Whatever could burn was gone. Whatever could not had tumbled into the city's streets and cellars. As far as the eye could see, only ruins and ashes remained.

The impact of the dreadful scene seemed to sap Irene's strength. Slowly, wearily, she turned away. Tears welled in her eyes. It would be a long walk home.

In a short time the whole world learned about the fire and its terrible toll. Three hundred people had died in the flames. Almost three and a half square miles had been leveled. More than seventeen thousand buildings had been destroyed, with a loss of $200 million. Some people were convinced that the once-great city would remain forever a skeleton—forever a charred reminder of the unimaginable fire. But such people didn't reckon with the spirit of Chicago's citizens. Those who visit Chicago today look upon far more than the ghost of a once-proud city. Instead, they gaze with admiration at a city rebuilt to a new level of splendor.

Should you visit Chicago, just glance around at the towering skyscrapers and busy streets. As you stand there, let your imagination wander back to the year 1871. Look into the distance. Maybe the Chicago skyline will take on an eerie orange glow. Perhaps—just for a moment—you'll see that dreadful storm of fire approaching, just as it did on that windy October night—so many years ago.